To Heal a Nation

52 Weeks of Meditations to Heal Our Nation and Ourselves

Kathleen Miritello

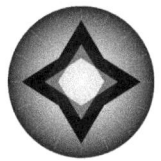

Copyright © 2012 by Energy Works LLC

Front cover photograph courtesy of Brian Fillman

Back cover photograph courtesy of Debra Richards of Richards Studio of Photography

Graphic artistry by Cynthia Fillman of Intuitive Design

Edited by Daniel P. Kray

All rights reserved. No part of this book may be reproduced in any form by any electronic or mechanical means including photocopying, recording, or information storage and retrieval, without permission in writing from the publisher.

Printed in the United States of America

First printing: 2012

ISBN 978-0-9885361-0-4

Table of Contents

Introduction i
Acknowledgement iii
Meditation Instructions 1
Meditation Topics 5
Index 109

Introduction

This is a book for the spiritually-minded regardless of one's particular religious affiliation (or lack of affiliation). All it requires is a sincere belief in what some call God, others refer to as Spirit or a Universal power, and ultimately our connection to this divine source.

I readily admit to being an unabashed patriot. A good portion of my life has been spent in either military or civilian public sector service. This has given me the opportunity to literally travel the globe and left me with an even greater appreciation for all this great nation offers to those with rights of her citizenship. I love my country not only because I was born and raised here but also from having seen the oppression that can result from the absence of democracy. That said, our nation is increasingly beleaguered by crises brought on either internally by a growing sense of rancor among our political parties or externally from the threat of terrorism.

I am not fond of protests and demonstrations. To me, they smack of cursing the darkness rather than "lighting a candle" to paraphrase John F. Kennedy's famously inspiring speech. Instead, in looking at the challenges that face our nation I believe in the power of prayer to help us overcome the obstacles in our path. My hope is that this book may help light a candle and contribute in some small way to our nation's future being a bit brighter and more promising than it might otherwise be. This book is about the power of prayer and meditation to bring healing and assist in strengthening and protecting our nation. We can accomplish only so much through diplomacy, treaties, negotiations, and the use or threat of military force. The rest comes from prayer.

The meditations described herein do not need to be done in any particular order and can begin at any point in the year. Presuming, with firmly held optimism that our country and this book will both exist for many, many years to come, I would hope these writings continue to bring benefit to our nation.*

*For a weekly source of additional meditations please go to my site, www.meditationproject.blogspot.com or *Like* "The Meditation Project" page on Facebook.

Acknowledgement

*To my teachers, Reverend Rosalyn L. Bruyere,
Ken Weintrub, and Reverend Jennifer Halls,
whose patience, good humor, wisdom, and encouragement
have helped to show me the light;*

*and to Dion Fortune,
whose spiritual work during World War II
sparked a lasting flame of inspiration
for many such as myself who never knew her.*

Meditation Instructions

For those who may be asking themselves, "How do I meditate?" the answer is the perhaps unsatisfying response that there is no one correct way. Just as there are varieties of ways in which people pray, so do people meditate using many different methods.

Some simple things to consider include finding a time, place, and position that are comfortable for you. Some people like to pray or meditate first thing in the morning and others like to make it their last activity of the day before climbing into bed. You can meditate standing, lying down, sitting, or even walking – whatever best suits you. It is helpful to meditate in an area where you aren't distracted, so perhaps finding a quiet space away from the television or the chatter of family members will make you more able to focus.

In the beginning you may believe it is necessary to silence the incessant barrage of thoughts that want to carom through your head. However, you will quickly find this can be a maddeningly frustrating objective. Rather than trying to silence your mind just let any thoughts or feelings occur while you adopt the neutrality of an objective observer. Let the thoughts come and go without feeling any sense of failure that you aren't exerting better control over them. Soon you will discover the gaps between the thoughts become longer and more frequent, and before you know it you've achieved that long sought-after experience of inner serenity. As for how long to meditate – start slow, perhaps only trying to find that inner quietness for a single minute, then build up gradually to whatever time feels right to you.

One important principle of meditation is to recognize that it is as much a physical activity as a mental activity. For the meditations described in this book to positively impact our world we want to feel in our body the unique quality represented by each meditation topic. Select a topic at random or begin at the front or back of the book and with each theme ask yourself how that particular attribute feels to you. When you experience that trait or characteristic how does it make you feel? Hold that sensation in your body and let it resonate as you focus on the meditation issue. Think of your body as an antenna that is broadcasting the message of that topic out into the world. Then one by one, gradually spreading across each community we will help heal this country and in the process bring the blessing of a healing to our own lives as well.

Week One

Possibility

The actor Christopher Reeve once said,

> "So many of our dreams at first seem impossible, then they seem improbable, and then, when we summon the will, they soon become inevitable."

We all too often limit our accomplishments by predetermining what we think is possible and subsequently acting as though that restriction held true. Numerous acclaimed feats were achieved mainly due to a blessed ignorance of limitations. A 2006 book by Nando Parrado and Vince Rause titled, "Miracle in the Andes," about the 1972 air disaster in which a Uruguayan rugby team became stranded in the rugged terrain of the Andes tells of one survivor who managed to walk across the mountains into Chile to contact rescuers. Afterward, people found it incredible to realize that he had accomplished this heroic task. With no training, no equipment, and only the barest of provisions he managed to navigate his way over peaks and cliffs that would challenge professional mountain climbers. It was a feat he should not have been able to carry out, and had he realized the trial before him he may not have even tried. But his ignorance of the difficulty and strong desire to survive pushed him to make the attempt. In our own lives we want to examine this week not what is probable for us to achieve based on what we think are our capabilities. Instead, let us seek to expand beyond our limitations and summon the will to reach for what is held in the broader realm of possibility. Additionally, let us consider what may be possible for this wonderful country if we pull together and work to achieve what is in our higher interests.

Week Two

Discipline

There is a common misconception that people who are considered religious martyrs or saints had somehow attained a state of "perfection" in life. We tend to think of them as strong individuals who never wavered in their path and therefore experienced none of the weaknesses and temptations that litter the path of the rest of us mere mortals. A 2010 book by Eric Metaxas on the martyred German pastor, Diedrich Bonhoeffer ("Bonhoeffer: Pastor, Martyr, Prophet, Spy"), dispels this illusion. Prior to his imprisonment Bonhoeffer was occasionally prone to spells of depression, yet in letters to friends while incarcerated he reassured them he did not find himself plagued by this in the least. Numerous witnesses during the time of his imprisonment by the Nazis have attested to the immense feeling of calm that characterized Bonhoeffer, even during such terrifying moments as when the prison where he was being held was subjected to Allied bombing raids. He gave credit to his source of strength in the discipline he maintained of daily prayer and meditation, the reading of the Bible, and the singing of favorite German hymns. As Metaxas puts it, "So Bonhoeffer was not 'naturally' strong and courageous. His equanimity was the result of self-discipline, of deliberately turning to God." In our prayer and meditation let us consider in what manner we may benefit and gain strength from added discipline in our life. Is there perhaps some practice we want to maintain more consistently that would help us mentally, physically, or spiritually? In addition, let us consider how our nation would benefit from greater discipline and where that is most needed as we look to the future of this great country.

Week Three

Community

Modern life and all the conveniences it brings has gradually contributed to a weakening of the once important family unit. Present-day transportation and communication capabilities make it more common for families to be geographically dispersed. With this change comes the loss of an embedded support network that used to exist within the extended family. As a result, people can feel isolated and alone when they have needs they can't meet on their own. Rather than looking to the government to become our social surrogate we want to increase people's willingness to generate their own support networks in the communities where they live, work, or go to school. There are individuals around us whose needs can be met simply by offering a social network of caring people to which they can turn. Who and where are they? If we foster this sense of looking out for each other we strengthen our community ties and become healthier as a nation. This week in our meditation we want to enhance people's willingness to lend assistance to those around them and build a greater desire for community among the people of this nation.

Week Four

Stewardship

No matter which metric you choose (per capita income, Gross National Product, etc.), this nation ranks as a very powerful force globally. One wonders if our Founding Fathers had any notion as to how influential and powerful a country we would become. With the immense resources and power we possess, however, comes an equally important burden of responsibility in how we exercise that influence. Those around us with less ability or fewer resources naturally become our charges. As "good stewards" we need to care for those charges and should accept that responsibility willingly and gladly. When we act as a "good steward" it can serve to reflect our gratitude for the abundance of blessings we have received. Even in these strained financial times people need to retain their capacity to be generous with others. It would be easy to rationalize the desire to be miserly and to adopt the hoarding mentality that followed the Great Depression. Instead, we want to instill an awareness of the abundance that still exists in this great nation and a capability for people to give when needed. No matter how much loss we may be experiencing as a result of crises occurring around us there is always the ability to share what we have with others. We want to spread that willing spirit of generosity and stewardship among the people of this nation and in doing so reduce the disparity between those who have and those who are in want. Let us foster a desire to take on the responsibility of stewardship in recognition and gratitude for all that we abundantly possess.

Week Five

Hope

The beginning of each new year brings with it so much promise and potential. However, it often seems as though the media only wants to talk about the latest crisis, financial or otherwise, and to perpetuate in the nation's consciousness a "doom and gloom" mentality. With the constant bombardment of such negativity it is easy to understand how some become discouraged, coming to believe not only that things will never improve but they can only get worse. Such a mentality can be contagious, bringing a darkness that wants to seep into every corner and snuff out any glimmer of hope that tries to arise. This contagion leaves individuals feeling trapped, eventually resulting in their surrender to the hopelessness that surrounds them. However, we can counterbalance this stifling negativity by working instead to infuse a sense of optimism and hope in our populace. What will help our country achieve its dreams is to increase the feeling of hope in its residents. We want to create a positive expectation that conditions are capable of getting better. It won't be easy and will take time, but given the tremendous potential of this nation and its resources we have the capability to overcome any challenge or difficulty. Yes, our nation will always have significant challenges before her, but if we come together and put collective energy into supporting our country we have a much better chance of seeing things improve. Truly, with hope all things are possible for this great nation.

Week Six

Altruism

Every year the nation pauses to commemorate Martin Luther King, Jr. who offered the following inspirational quote:

> "Never, never be afraid to do what's right, especially if the well-being of a person or animal is at stake. Society's punishments are small compared to the wounds we inflict on our soul when we look the other way."

This speaks to the themes of courage, the need to step up and take action, concern for the welfare of others – all of which is summarized in the one concept of altruism. To be altruistic implies putting the needs of others before one's own. In this stance, it may require us to place ourselves in the firing line of criticism from society when we go against the flow to defend or help another person. This can be difficult to do, but it is even more difficult when you fail to do something and turn away instead. Bullying has become such a common occurrence in our schools, and it can result in lingering feelings of guilt at not speaking up to defend those who become the target of harassment. Even if the bullying is not physical in nature, one can clearly be psychologically bullied. Someone who is a perfectly nice individual may be perceived as having some quirk or oddity that serves as a magnet for persecution by one's peers. With the continuing prevalence of such behavior not only in our schools but in so many places in society we want to bolster our willingness to be altruistic and especially to step up to defend others when needed. This week in our meditation efforts let us ask that throughout this country people embrace altruism and act with more concern for each other.

Week Seven

Service

Many of our political leaders in the past have called the citizens of this nation to service. John F. Kennedy did it most memorably when he delivered his stirring inauguration speech on January 20, 1961. In it he declared,

> "And so, my fellow Americans: ask not what your country can do for you - ask what you can do for your country. My fellow citizens of the world: ask not what America will do for you, but what together we can do for the freedom of man. Finally, whether you are citizens of America or citizens of the world, ask of us the same high standards of strength and sacrifice which we ask of you. With a good conscience our only sure reward, with history the final judge of our deeds, let us go forth to lead the land we love,

asking His blessing and His help, but knowing that here on earth God's work must truly be our own."

The need for service is just as important today as it was in 1961. Given the magnitude of the challenges facing our nation we cannot rely on the efforts of government alone to restore this nation's health. It will take willingness on the part of every person at all levels to offer assistance and aid in service to others. Whether it is contributing time, money, resources, or prayer all must look around themselves and see where they are called to bring their light. In doing so, we stand a better chance of a speedier recovery from our country's ills.

Week Eight

Inspiration

The need for inspiration goes far beyond an artist or writer seeking to find his or her creative Muse. Our elected officials require more inspiration in order to come up with solutions that will help our nation recover from the pressures of the current economic situation. Business people could use more inspiration to find innovative ways to improve efficiency without resorting to out-sourcing that takes needed jobs outside the U.S. Teachers benefit from inspiration when they find a way to motivate a child or come up with an effective method to help their students understand a complex concept. Even in our day-to-day living inspiration can add an element of creativity, enthusiasm, and motivation that helps us with challenging tasks. When you consider great accomplishments, the impetus that often drove someone to aim for higher achievement is inspiration. This week in our prayer and meditation let us consider whether there are aspects to our life that could benefit from greater inspiration. Additionally, let us ask that our elected officials, business leaders, teachers, and all people find themselves filled with the inspiration that will improve their work and life.

Week Nine

Light

Each year as our nation prepares to celebrate July 4th, our Independence Day, hearts and eyes turn to the Statue of Liberty as a symbol of what our country represents. While she stands for several ideals – the offer of welcome to immigrants seeking refuge and the promise of freedom and opportunity – this week we want her image as a symbol of light to serve as our inspiration. Years ago when immigrants came here by boat she was often the first view they had of our country as their ships drew near to Ellis Island. Her torch held aloft greeted them and raised their spirits at the end of what was likely an arduous journey. Today she continues to encourage people to recognize what is good about our country and all that it represents as a model of democracy. We therefore want to use Lady Liberty's torch to serve as a beacon of illumination for our country. Let us begin with our neighborhoods, our communities, our towns and cities, and ask that the areas in which we live be filled with her light. Let us look around us and find those areas that may be struggling against the darkness of apathy, of hopelessness, and of despair, and ask that they instead be filled with a light that brings hope, optimism, and a promise of a better future. From shore to shore and border to border let the entire nation be filled with this brilliant, undiluted light that will serve to amplify the best and highest qualities of our country and the people who live across its vast lands.

Week Ten

Kindness

One of the lessons emphasized by world-renowned healer and spiritual teacher, Reverend Rosalyn L. Bruyere, is that our culture today places more importance on intellect than on simple courtesy. One need look no further for an example than so-called entertainment in the form of situation comedies in which characters score points with the audience by wittily tearing down another person. Even in normal discourse one is perceived as being unsophisticated if you are unable to articulate with surgical precision what is wrong with another's ideas. Rev. Bruyere once challenged a class of her students by asking, "Would you rather be smart or kind?" Some immediately questioned how you could be considered smart if he or she didn't also know to be kind. There is no reason the two must remain mutually exclusive, but an imbalance appears to have developed in our society where people are given more kudos for their intellect than their kindness. Years ago a popular bumper sticker began to be seen in which a phrase referring to the senseless acts of mayhem that would often make the evening news was altered to instead encourage people to "Practice Random Acts of Kindness." While it may appear to be a simple philosophy, it bears a weightier potential in helping to right what is wrong with our society. This week in our prayer and meditation let us ask what acts of kindness we could contribute to the world around us. Let us also use our prayer to help promote the notion that the quality of kindness be better appreciated and emulated and thereby improve our nation as a whole.

Week Eleven

Determination

It is almost unfathomable today to conceive what our forefathers faced in taking the momentous step of leaving England on a perilous journey across the ocean to forge new lives for themselves in an unknown land. Truly this was a leap of faith for those who chose to leave the comfort of familiar surroundings in the hope of a better way of life. One can only imagine how easily they succumbed to bouts of self-doubt, questioning whether they had made the right move. To carry out their plans must have demanded incredible courage and confidence that things would turn out right. Similarly, the heroes who have served and sometimes fallen for our country clearly were required to face tremendous challenges. Fortunately for the rest of us, our honored veterans had the tenacity to firmly take action when others might choose to turn their backs. This is not about the rightness or wrongness of war. That is something better left to debates elsewhere. It is about the resoluteness of one's character that drives one to act with firmness of purpose under difficult conditions. Just as these veterans and forefathers found the courage to act purposefully, so do we as citizens of this nation want to find that same determination in our everyday lives. Even though our nation's present challenges seems far less daunting by comparison we still are on a precipice before the uncertain future. As we strive to find our way we want to summon the same level of determination and the unshakable belief that we are moving in the right direction. In possessing such determination it will keep us from wavering from the course we need to take.

Week Twelve

Faith

Many different belief systems embrace the concept of free will and the choices we are allowed to make throughout our life. Presumably we bring the possible negative or positive consequences of our choices to mind before carrying out an action. However, there are times when we have to trust that the outcome will not go awry. For example, accepting a new job that requires a move to another part of the country or a total career change can test our level of conviction. Ultimately, however, you have to act confidently with faith. Each time you act a multitude of possible outcomes exist, some of which you might anticipate and others of which may never occur to you beforehand. Rather than be paralyzed into non-action by the fear of what could go wrong you want to instead choose to behave with faith, asking that the highest good be the outcome of one's actions. As a country we want to similarly ask that our national actions be taken in the faith that the highest and best good will result.

Week Thirteen

Triumph

There is a Nike commercial that played during the 2010 Olympics and showed a montage of athletes who faced potential defeat but continued on despite the momentary setback. The ad slogan proclaimed that a real winner is defined by how quickly someone gets back up. You certainly don't have to be a competitive athlete to experience adversity in your life – everyone does sooner or later. Perhaps you can think back to moments when you faced a crisis or had to weather a period of turmoil and hardship in your life. Looking back reflectively you may be able to identify some positive benefit that you took away from the experience. A book titled, "Deep Survival," by Laurence Gonzales describes people who overcame amazing odds when faced with true peril and managed to survive. The common characteristics they all possessed were the ability to overcome any desire to give up, the optimism to believe there had to be a way out, and the fortitude to keep seeking a resolution. In our meditation this week we want to reflect on where we have been successful in achieving triumph over adversity and to bring what we have learned from the experience into our character so we overcome the next hurdle we face. At the same time, consider what challenges our own country has had to meet and what is needed for us to triumph as a nation going forward.

Week Fourteen

Resolve

During World War II, a British woman named Dion Fortune, who was the founder of an esoteric spiritual order known as the Society of Inner Light, chose to use the prayer and meditation resources of her group to help bolster her nation's resolve against Hitler. While it is now almost unimaginable, at the time there was a great deal of controversy among nations as to the position they should take with regard to Hitler. Some believed they needed to stand up to the Nazis while others just as firmly believed they should capitulate in order to limit their losses and presumably receive more lenient treatment in return. Dion Fortune felt her country was losing its resolve to fight against the evil of the Axis powers and recruited the members of her order to pray for the country in order to sustain their ability to resist. She knew if they lost their resolve the repercussions would be momentous and irreversible. There are times in our own lives when we can easily feel overwhelmed by the magnitude of a problem and be tempted to give up instead. By asking for an increase in resolve this week we want to examine where we may need additional support to overcome a difficult stretch. Additionally, we want to look to the future of our country and ask that our nation's resolve be made firm to see our way through any trials that await us.

Week Fifteen

Optimism

In Dion Fortune's spiritual work during World War II, described in the book, "The Magical Battle of Britain," she discusses the importance of realizing the impact we have on those around us. At a time when the periodic bombings of London resulted in prolonged moments of terror and chaos she noted how the atmosphere at the headquarters for their spiritual society instead resonated with a sense of peace. She exhorted her members to "act 'as if' what we want to believe is true, and we shall find that we have very likely brought it into manifestation." More importantly, she realized that their group served as a nucleus for the nation in maintaining a spirit of stability and serenity. This notion goes far beyond mere "positive thinking" but is firmly rooted in an awareness of the divine assistance and protection that is always available to us. As our nation readies itself for the future there are those who would like to broadcast a message of pessimism. There is nothing at all that pessimism contributes in trying to improve a situation. To help restore some balance in the nation we want to use ourselves as beacons of light to manifest illumination and optimism. As we move through our world let us remember that in subtle ways we alter those whom we encounter. This week we focus on broadcasting a sense of optimism that will ultimately inspire others to strive for progress rather than remain captive to fear and hopelessness.

Week Sixteen

Humility

When true humility is present it signifies the acknowledgement that there is something greater than yourself. In the absence of humility your actions are driven by ego, and this becomes a common source of discord and unrest. Think about how many wars and other violent acts over the centuries have been motivated by ego. If only those whose actions were prompted by ego could have instead recognized a desire for humility these conflicts may never have occurred. While some might say humility reflects how insignificant we are it can also be seen to reflect the grandeur of the universe and acknowledge that we are a part of that. Rather than emphasizing worthlessness it fosters a sense that we are actually greater for contributing in a small way to the vastness around us. By embracing humility your motivations are extended beyond the limitations of our own little sphere of being.

We are able instead to embrace and support actions that benefit a larger whole. In our meditation this week we want to ask that true humility be encouraged in our own thoughts and actions. At the same time please ask that greater humility be extended across this nation.

Week Seventeen

Passion

Passion is a key aspect of our vitality. When we are passionate about something it often drives us to take action and can move us in a different direction from where we are now. With each quadrennial occurrence of the Olympic Games there are many opportunities to witness passion as athletes from all across the globe meet to try and perform at their very best on a world platform. Given the dedication and sacrifice required for these athletes to accomplish what they do, passion for their sport must be at the core of what motivates them. As we watch these young people strive to excel we want to also examine where we feel passion in our own lives. What pushes us to improve the way we behave as conscientious human beings? What truly motivates us to become better people, seeking to evolve rather than devolve through this life? Additionally, we want to examine how our own country is perceived in terms of its passions. Rather than being seen as a nation infatuated with celebrities and professional athletes we want to be recognized as having passion for such issues as human rights, decency, and peaceful diplomacy. In our prayer and meditation let us ask that our country embrace with passion the desire to become even better in all that we do and represent.

Week Eighteen

Joy

In our meditation this week we want to focus on appreciating all that is present in life that deserves to be celebrated and rejoiced. Among people who have survived the most difficult of circumstances there is a quality that goes beyond mere optimism – it is the ability to find that which makes them cherish each moment of being alive. When you think about how miraculous life is to begin with and then consider the incredible complexity and intricacy of how our bodies work there is something to be celebrated just in how truly extraordinary we are as corporeal beings. Even for those with any variety of mental or physical challenges, such as those who may be in chronic pain, there is some facet of life's continuing experience that can be cherished. If you can discover what this aspect is that makes you feel alive it will resonate through your body and communicate a sense of joy to those around you. By filling this nation with a stronger sense of joy it will also make us more resilient as a people to weather any difficult times.

Week Nineteen

Groundedness

Our society is often too focused on the quality of one's intellect as a measure of how advanced we have become. As a result of being so focused on what goes on in our head, we no longer have an appreciation for the importance of being connected to the energy of the earth through our feet. Staying connected and grounded helps sustain our individual energy level. There is a limitless source of energy always present at our feet that we often fail to recognize. Instead, we deplete ourselves by rushing around putting out the "fires" that flare up around us. People who remain rooted firmly to the ground seem better at weathering various crises. Being grounded helps to maintain a healthier and more balanced perspective on what is truly important in life and what can be ignored. Reconnecting with a sense of being rooted into the earth will help this nation draw on an important source of strength and allow us to keep a clearer perspective to weather the occasional turmoil around us.

Week Twenty

Resourcefulness

Many communities across our country are becoming more "green" or ecologically-minded. For example, many people now seek to buy groceries such as produce and meats that are locally grown and harvested not only to support small farming but to also save on the fuel and expense needed to transport food long distances. It is also becoming increasingly common for supermarkets to no longer make plastic bags available and instead encourage customers to carry reusable totes. Unfortunately, our use of non-biodegradable plastic over the years has led to the formation of what is referred to as a "floating garbage dump" in the Pacific Ocean. The ocean currents have naturally collected the mostly plastic remnants into a huge "island" that some speculate to be as large as twice the size of Texas. The full impact of this much plastic on the fish, mammals, and organisms that live in the ocean is immeasurable, but it obviously cannot be positive. In order to prevent this and other similar damage from continuing we need to more resourcefully find alternative ways to undertake daily life with a smaller carbon footprint. It may mean bringing your own container to your favorite coffee house rather than getting a one-use disposable cup or bringing your own bags to the grocery store instead of accepting plastic ones. This week in our prayer and meditation let us examine how we want to increase our resourcefulness out of respect for the planet and in acknowledgement that its natural resources are both limited and precious.

Week Twenty-One

Equilibrium

This week in our prayer and meditation we want to focus on the relationship between equilibrium and justice. A state of equilibrium implies there are opposing forces that cancel each other out to achieve a neutral or balanced condition. When we think of justice we all too often consider it to be achieved when the outcome agrees with our viewpoint or position on an issue. However, the force of equilibrium implies there will be instances when the outcome is dissonant with what we may desire. We need to accept that there are times when the way our laws are carried out appears uneven. Consider though how the pendulum must swing in both directions, not just in one, for true balance to occur. In looking at our lives and in considering the events in our nation we want to accept that what may appear to be a transitory moment of imbalance is merely the movement necessary within a dynamic state.

Let us trust that conditions never remain static at one extreme or the other but will ultimately find a balancing point of equilibrium.

Week Twenty-Two

Dedication

To be dedicated to something, such as a project or cause, sometimes requires that you reprioritize or even subordinate your own personal ambitions in order to achieve the greater goal at hand. To be dedicated implies a commitment to something in which you believe, often over a length of time. It is a belief so deep and abiding that it alters your behavior and can reprioritize your goals and objectives as to how you want to carry out your life. Life-changing events can lead to a powerful sense of dedication to a particular cause. For instance, organizations such as Mothers Against Drunk Driving (MADD) began when the tragic loss of a family member spurred relatives to prevent these tragedies from recurring. Their resulting dedication to this cause significantly altered their lives. Each of us likewise may feel a sense of dedication to something in life. Those who do feel such an obligation find it highly motivating and even inspirational to commit to something they believe in so firmly. This week in our meditation we want to look at the commitments we have made and see what they say about how we have prioritized our life goals. Are we dedicated to those things that reflect our higher purpose, or do we need to perhaps restructure the way we have focused our time and effort? In our meditation we also want to examine the commitments made by this country and ask that they, too, come to reflect our highest goals as a nation. Let us foster across this nation a sense of dedication to those principles that will help our country continue to progress in the right direction.

Week Twenty-Three

Courage

Numerous feats of courage repeatedly affirm that many of the heroes whose exploits we hear about behave not with fearlessness but act despite the fear they feel. In situations that would reasonably drive most people into the latter two states of the "fight, flight, or freeze" response those who act with courage feel the same threat but push themselves to take action anyway. In some individuals this response pattern is almost instinctive, but in others it can be embedded or learned through conscious intent. In each instance in which you identify a fearful situation and summon the courage to act anyway it expands your abilities and diminishes your limitations. Network television has aired one of those "hidden camera" programs that use actors to create what appear to be real situations. The premise for the show is to present an ethical dilemma for those who are bystanders and see how they behave. It is insightful to see how people react, or more often than not, failed to react. Those who ultimately take action by speaking up or confronting the actors are then let in on the true nature of the situation. In their subsequent on-camera debriefing they frequently state they felt a reluctance to interfere but were motivated to do something. While perhaps on a lesser scale than running into a burning building, the same behavioral incentive is present – they acted even in the presence of an initial aversion to respond because they knew it was the right thing to do. In our meditation this week we want to examine our own lives and identify where a fear may be present that is holding us back. Let us instead begin to alter our response pattern by consciously summoning the courage needed to deal with the situation and ultimately expand our capabilities.

Week Twenty-Four

Pride

Each year as our nation pauses during the Memorial Day holiday to commemorate our service men and women who gave their lives for their country, the occasion prompts us to consider all the things for which we can be proud about the United States. This country has been a popular target for media bashing, both domestically and abroad, yet the negatives are vastly outweighed by many more positives that seldom generate news headlines. For instance, as a nation Americans give twice as much as the next most charitable country, topping the list with a donation level of 1.7 percent of our gross domestic product. This compares to the second most charitable country in the world, Great Britain, at 0.73 percent. On another level, we seem to take for granted the privileges and freedoms afforded men and women alike in America. One only need travel to countries where women are subjected to oppressive restrictions and abuse with little recourse to protection from authorities to make one grateful and proud of the equality we experience here. The list of admirable qualities appears limitless – the strength of our industries, the excellence of higher education, the availability and quality of medical care, the right of all citizens to vote, and on and on. This week in our prayer and meditation if we take time to reflect on the qualities that make us most proud of our nation we can help elevate and strengthen those characteristics even more.

Week Twenty-Five

Foresight

To have foresight in one's actions means that you take the future into consideration and act in a manner that makes you more prepared to deal with what will come. It requires us to think about the future consequences of our actions before we do something. New parents who realize some day their son or daughter will want to attend college begin saving for such an event in the very early years of that child's life. Those who are trying to live more ecologically-minded lives realize the implications of continuing to use up a finite supply of natural resources, and they modify their behavior now to try to lessen the impact on the planet. Financial experts advise workers to begin saving in an investment fund as soon as possible and not wait until you near retirement to begin planning for that stage in your life. In each instance action is taken today that may only reap benefits decades later. It is therefore easy to put off taking such action today, feeling you have plenty of time before being forced to proceed. However, acting with foresight of the consequences makes the future event a significantly easier experience. This week in our prayer and meditation let us consider the future in the decisions we make today as a nation. Let us ask to have sufficient foresight so that when the future comes we will find ourselves better prepared as a country to deal with whatever presents itself.

Week Twenty-Six

Ambition

Ambition is a concept that unfortunately has become sullied by those who have focused on misdirected goals or objectives. To have ambition is to strive for something and to be motivated to be successful in achieving that goal. The key is to make certain it is a worthy and just goal as are the means used in its pursuit. Through honorable ambition we seek true transformation; when we form lofty aims they can lift us above our present state. If we are to succeed in our desire for transformation we must have ambition. That is what provides the impetus for the initial movement needed for change and is what keeps us on the path even when it becomes difficult to follow. In our meditation this week we want to examine where in our own lives our ambition is directed. Are we focused on a right and just goal, and are we using the proper means to stay on the path in order to achieve a successful transformation? In addition, consider our country's ambitions and ask that they, too, be aligned with the right goals for us to transform and evolve as a nation.

Week Twenty-Seven

Authenticity

A few years ago an independent video titled, "A Reminder of the Important Things in Life," quickly went viral across the Internet's social networks. [To see the video follow this link: http://tinyurl.com/2ue69lp.] It is short, less than 3 minutes in length, but contains a number of valuable reminders, many of which relate to this week's theme of authenticity. To be authentic means to be true to yourself despite the pressure of external influences of family, friends, and living in a material world. This presumes, however, that you are in touch with knowing who you truly are, something that is not an easy task and for most of us a lifelong pursuit. Even then, there are pressures to conform, to go along with the crowd, and to "fit in." Each of these can be an obstacle if we allow them to pull us off center of our true self. Instead, if we act from a place of authenticity we remain centered and grounded and are more likely to take the right action that doesn't compromise our principles and beliefs. This week we want to ask in our meditation that we be aided in acting with genuine authenticity and in remaining true to ourselves.

Week Twenty-Eight

Liberty

Each year we celebrate Independence Day, the July 4th holiday, and use this time to focus on the notion of liberty and freedom from oppression. The freedoms we possess by virtue of our national citizenship are often taken for granted. You only need to travel to other parts of the world to quickly realize others are not so fortunate. Yet even in a land where the roots of liberty are so deeply entrenched in our origins and history many of us fail to appreciate the significance of this hard-earned right. It was the impetus for our forefathers to leave the country of their birth and travel across an ocean to settle in a strange new land. Wars have been fought and lives lost to retain this right. In our meditation this week we want to express gratitude for the sacrifices that have been made to secure our freedoms and to instill an appreciation for the inalienable right of liberty.

Week Twenty-Nine

Truth

There have been numerous instances over our nation's history when prominent court cases ended in controversial conclusions, spurring public outrage. For example, in 1995 the criminal court trial of O.J. Simpson on the charges of having murdered his ex-wife, Nicole Brown Simpson, concluded with an astonishing acquittal. More recently, in July 2011, the Casey Anthony trial captivated much of the nation and followed the sad case of the disappearance and presumed murder of a young girl named Caylee, similarly ending with divisive results. In both instances some people felt a huge injustice had been done while others thought the tenets on which our legal system are based, such as the presumption of innocence until proven guilty and the need to establish guilt beyond a reasonable doubt, were validated. About the only thing everyone agrees on is that the one outcome the trials did not produce was the truth. The answers continue to elude most parties as to the exact circumstances of these individual's deaths. While it may be an altogether naïve and overly optimistic view some like to believe our legal system is founded on the principle of seeking the truth through as fair a procedure as possible. These cases are not the first time the legal process has resulted in a departure from that principle, and they certainly will not be the last. However, a hallmark of our nation is its reliance on a fair judicial system that is altogether absent in the barbarous way so-called justice is meted out in certain countries. For our justice system to continue to succeed we need to support its search for the truth through our prayers. This week in our prayer and meditation let us ask that courts at all levels across the nation be filled with the light of truth. May all individuals engaged in the legal system in those halls of justice be motivated to work tirelessly to find the truth, and may the energy of our prayers help to sustain them in their work.

Week Thirty

Commonality

Divisions and differences between various religions and countries continue through the eons to be all too apparent. For as long as different faiths and beliefs have existed it seems there has always been an accompanying strife that arises almost as a natural consequence. Yet it doesn't need to be this way. Rather than focusing on the differences and inevitably debating their relative merits, an alternative is to recognize what is held in common. When we distill most major religious systems down to what they hold as central we find the belief in a higher power, Supreme Being, or universal divine presence that is inclusive of all. This is not to advocate that all religious differences be abandoned and an über mega-religion be created in their place. Rather we want to promote the acceptance of those differences and more importantly acknowledge the presence of mutual core beliefs across religions. By focusing instead on what is held in common this may engender more respect for the differences and reduce the tension they seem to otherwise promote. In our meditation this week we want to ask that an appreciation for the commonality among different religions proliferate across this country and around the world.

Week Thirty-One

Virtue

In a recorded talk by Caroline Myss titled, "The Sacred Contract of America," she speaks of the mystic background of our nation's founders, many of whom were Freemasons. They believed that virtue was a necessary quality for a group of free people to govern themselves in this newly formed country. In the case of Freemasons virtue meant a sense of reverence for the qualities of loyalty and honor that help bind a group together and allows them to prevail over any difficulty. Myss bluntly acknowledges the excesses and foibles that have come to characterize this nation in more modern times and challenges us to work toward "refocusing that shadow toward the light." According to Myss, what distinguishes our country is that its origin, and therefore the purpose for its very existence, was created with a particular consciousness. When our founders created this nation of free people they knew our country would be called to a greatness that goes far beyond any exercise of military might or global diplomacy. We were created with a spiritual covenant that requires us to seek to operate more in the light than those we oppose. While we have strayed from what initially held us together we still have the extraordinary capability and resources to fulfill the promise conceived by our Founding Fathers. Rather than allow our challenges to drive us further apart we want to work through prayer toward an increased desire for the virtue that will sustain us through these difficulties. Let us ask in our prayer and meditation that we see a return to honor, loyalty, and virtue that extends across the country and helps us bring this nation back toward the light.

Week Thirty-Two

Empathy

Past measures of intelligence focused on such cognitive abilities as abstract reasoning, spatial imagery, word and sentence comprehension, etc. In more modern times, however, a new form of intelligence has come into prominence – one labeled as Emotional Intelligence. This refers to the ability to accurately identify the emotions of others as well as those feelings we ourselves experience. It is fundamental to our ability to understand and deal appropriately with others and in truly knowing ourselves. To have empathy implies you act with consideration for what others are feeling and how your behavior will impact them. Whether because of our increasing interaction with computer technology or some other factor, it seems as though the quality of empathy is waning in our society. Those who bully others, for instance, clearly lack the ability to appreciate how their actions can impact their victims. They seem to regard this behavior as entertainment with callous disregard for the damage it may cause. In our meditation this week we want to ask that people across this country gain a greater desire for empathy and consequently act with more consideration for others.

Week Thirty-Three

Security

To make a country secure implies that we have reduced danger or eliminated the need for fear. However, more often than not the imposition of "security" measures has the contrary result and makes people feel more fearful and threatened. When you think about it, there is nothing that could ever guarantee anyone's total security. However, all too often people feel that they would be more secure if they only had a larger bank account, a better job, the right car or home, or the perfect relationship. Nevertheless, there are instances when someone in a Job-like string of misfortunes loses everything he possesses yet is later able to resurrect himself. Clearly whatever served as the basis for his previous notion of security was in error. In our meditation this week we want to examine what in our own lives is really needed for us to feel secure and reduce our anxiety about what the future may bring. Let us ponder what is at the core of our being and essential for us to feel secure and not threatened by the unexpected. Additionally, let us consider what is of fundamental importance for this nation to feel a sense of security. The answers may surprise us and reveal what is truly important in our lives.

Week Thirty-Four

Forgiveness

A powerful documentary released in 2006 titled, "Forgiving Dr. Mengele," is about a woman named Eva Mozes Kor who was born in Romania and became a Holocaust survivor. At the age of ten she and her twin sister lost all of their family members in Auschwitz. Eva and her sister were kept alive to serve as subjects for horrible medical experiments by the Nazis. They somehow survived, but the most miraculous part of her story is her subsequent choice to publicly forgive those who had tortured her and murdered her family. Fifty years after she was liberated from Auschwitz, Eva returned to the infamous site and publicly announced to the world that she forgave the Nazis for what they had done to her. It was a courageous act that subjected her to much criticism from fellow Holocaust survivors. As noted in The Forgiveness Project web site (www.theforgivenessproject.com) forgiveness is "the mental and/or spiritual process of relinquishing resentment, indignation or anger against another person for a perceived offense, or ceasing to demand punishment." It is an act of moving on and of freeing yourself from remaining a victim. So many of the conflicts in our own nation, in our relationships with others, and particularly around the world seem to arise from a desire for retribution. When we harbor these feelings of anger and victimization we only further harm ourselves. In our meditation and prayer this week we want to ask that the anger that seems to pervade our society and relationships be replaced with calm acceptance that what is past is past, and for the strength of character to extend true forgiveness to those who may have wronged us. If we can permeate this sense of forgiveness across our nation we will heal ourselves and quiet the discord that too frequently erupts.

Week Thirty-Five

Effort

Eleanor Roosevelt once said,

> "Surely, in the light of history, it is more intelligent to hope rather than to fear, to try rather than not to try. For one thing we know beyond all doubt: Nothing has ever been achieved by a person who says, 'It can't be done.'"

Such words encourage us to step out of our doubt and uncertainty to make the effort needed to take on a challenge we might otherwise forego. Whether it is fear of failure or feeling overwhelmed by a seemingly insurmountable task, there are so many potential obstacles that can prevent us from tackling a difficult endeavor. Yet inaction most certainly dooms us to failure, for we are held back from even making that initial attempt. In our meditation this week we want to ask where in our life we may be avoiding that first step and making the effort required to take on a daunting challenge. Let us further consider where in this nation we may also need to apply more effort to carry through on a task we have begun.

Week Thirty-Six

Prosperity

Sometimes people attach a particular stigma to being wealthy. In some circles it can be viewed as immoral to have accumulated wealth and possessions. Certainly this can be the case if done at the expense of others or gained through dishonest means, but achieving a particular status or level of material comfort is not in and of itself inherently despicable. It can help create or support a degree of philanthropy that might not otherwise exist. When your physical and material needs are met abundantly it also can provide a freedom of choice and action that allows you to volunteer your time and services. Or you might pursue a different career path that leads you to help others in a way that wouldn't be possible without the independence afforded by ample resources. Rather than malign or disparage someone for having achieved a measure of wealth, perhaps we would be better served to hold a more neutral view. After all, if we despise prosperity there is little likelihood we can ever attract it to our own lives. While not advocating the pursuit of wealth for wealth's sake, we may want to reconsider our view of prosperity and recognize that there is much good that can come from it. Instead of feeling envy or animosity toward those who have prosperity if we instead focus on increasing our own sense of generosity we may find it ultimately returned a hundredfold. This week in our meditation let us ask to be shown how to embrace and receive prosperity in our own lives in a way that may benefit our higher selves and this nation.

Week Thirty-Seven

Resilience

Each year our nation commemorates the anniversary of the lives lost in the terror attacks at the World Trade Center, the Pentagon, and a field in Shanksville, Pennsylvania. In these commemorations we want to acknowledge not the evil behind the events but the power of the human spirit to overcome unfathomable sorrow. With each precious year that passes since that event those who remain are robbed of time not able to be spent with friends, colleagues, husbands, wives, sons, daughters, brothers, sisters, fathers, and mothers. Yet, somehow, lives do go on. Amidst all the recollections of the event are those who have been able to move forward, and in living their lives their stories speak volumes about the resilience of human nature. Moving forward does not necessarily mean putting something entirely behind you, and it certainly does not mean forgetting. It means not allowing the pain and anguish to hold such a firm grasp on one's life that you remain frozen in time. Summoning the spirit of resilience gives a vital first nod to the awareness that gradually things will get better. It makes room for hope and eventually the return of even some joy into your life. More importantly, resilience prevents other more negative feelings such as anger and hatred from consuming your spirit. Even against the backdrop of continued threats to our security, across this nation people honor the fallen from years past and in so doing demonstrate the resilience that is so characteristic of our country. In our prayer and meditation this week let us ask that the nation be completely filled with the spirit of resilience that brings healing, comfort, and courage to all.

Week Thirty-Eight

Connection

One of the wonderful contributions from the field of quantum physics is the demonstration of the interconnectedness of distant objects to each other. By raising our awareness that we can impact objects and beings separated from us in space it makes us more conscious of the power of our words and actions. It is also what some believe serves as the foundation for remote healing and the power of prayer. In generating the prayer or the healing intention and releasing that into the universe you create a ripple of energy that travels through space (and perhaps time), eventually washing like a wave over another individual and impacting their existence. Centuries before quantum physics came along Mahayana Buddhism first referred to this connectivity as "Indra's Net" – a virtual spider web that extends out, creating connections between all the other objects and beings in the universe. In our meditation this week we want to focus on raising awareness of the connection of all beings to each other. By doing so, we hope to make people more conscious of the impact of their thoughts, words, and actions on others and the world around them and to thereby be motivated to create a more positive influence.

Week Thirty-Nine

Self-Awareness

To be fully self-aware requires that you recognize the darker side of yourself that we often prefer not to admit exists. Our nation certainly has had its share of a dark past with the legacy of our treatment of indigenous peoples or the shame of slavery. Rather than ignore these flaws and pretend they never occurred real healing comes when we are able to acknowledge that they are a part of our history, albeit without question a more reprehensible aspect. It is through this acceptance that we ensure they remain in the past. Our awareness of these past blights drives us to vow never to return to such deplorable conduct. It is the same with individuals. We each have a dark side, some facet of our personality or character that we perhaps loathe or that makes us feel ashamed, something that we would definitely prefer others never knew about us. Yet, if we are to heal that inner blemish we must be honest in our self-appraisal and admit what we have done, even if only to ourselves. There is also an important role for forgiveness that is essential for healing to occur. To achieve this we need to first take the step of acknowledging that aspect of our inner self that is hidden from others in order to let go of it. This week in our meditation we want to look deep inside ourselves and bring to consciousness those parts we may dislike. This honest self-awareness then allows for real forgiveness and makes it possible for us to be more like the higher self we strive to become.

Week Forty

Trust

To have trust in another person implies there is the ability to relinquish control and know everything will be taken care of properly. It can be a scary step to genuinely trust another individual and not feel as though you have to remain in charge in order for things to be done correctly. Trust can also involve the sharing of something that is cherished or confidential and feeling confident it will remain protected. One condition for establishing trust is to have a sense of the absence of risk or negative consequence from placing trust in someone. Seldom, however, are we ever entirely assured of this. There are many times in life when we may have to trust blindly in order to act. We have choices to make and must select the one that seems best at the time. Being able to trust ultimately reflects the confidence that we are guided and protected by a divine being even in the presence of the unknown. As we move through our work, school, or personal activities this upcoming week let us seek to do so with a sense of trust, and as the saying reminds us, "Let go and let God."

Week Forty-One

Cooperation

Webster's Dictionary defines bipartisanship as "marked by or involving cooperation, agreement, and compromise between two major political parties." The concepts of cooperation and compromise are at the cornerstone of our form of government. To be truly compromising requires you to be conciliatory when appropriate but to also fairly and firmly express views that may be in opposition to those held by others. Both sides have to attempt an understanding of the other's perspective and to be willing to weigh its advantages or disadvantages against your own ideas before taking a position. At times, however, the representatives of our political parties seem to sink to new lows in the childish finger-pointing and expressions of pique aimed at placing blame on others rather than taking needed responsibility. Under such conditions it will be very difficult, if not impossible, for our nation to accomplish what must be done to restore our country's financial and moral health. In each instance our elected officials appear to have lost sight of their mandate to seek the highest good for the group they represent. To someone who has become unemployed and subsequently faces the potential loss of their home, or to a parent who deals with the unbearable pain of a child killed in a conflict overseas such conduct of our elected officials must seem absurd and insulting. In our meditation efforts let us remember that prayer is more than a petition in which we ask God or Spirit or the Universe for a favor. Prayer is energy, and when we send out a prayer with energy it impacts the world around us. Let us focus the energy of our prayers such that our elected officials be filled with the true spirit of compromise and cooperation. For them to best serve this nation we ask that they gain a deeper consideration for the quality of cooperation in their thoughts, words, and actions.

Week Forty-Two

Adaptability

There are so many changes being forced on people and industries across the nation during these difficult times. People who may have identified with a particular career path or profession suddenly find themselves out of work and have to learn a new skill set in order to gain meaningful employment. Similarly, there is a story about a successful business that decades ago manufactured feedbags for horses. Their feedbags were considered very well-made and were quite popular. No matter how great their product or the quality of their work, however, when the "horseless carriage" took over they had a choice to make. Either figure out a way to make feedbags for automobiles or re-tool what they did. In the course of re-inventing yourself you may need to examine what is holding you back from being resilient and adaptive. For this nation in particular there may be things we are clinging to that need to be discarded. There are likely "cobwebs" that need to be swept out so we can recreate what this country stands for and represents. If we are to progress and evolve as individuals and as a nation we want to figure out a way to regain our sense of adaptability.

Week Forty-Three

Influence

Whether we are consciously aware of it or not we have an impact on the world around us merely by the energy we carry in our bodies. The quality of this energetic field is transmitted in a ripple effect as we move through our environment. Just as a pebble thrown into a pond ultimately has an effect on the waters on the opposite shore, our energy likewise impacts everything around us. Einstein once said energy is never lost, it only becomes transferred to another form of energy. This is a thought that should give pause if you think about the "downstream" impact of an angry moment and what happens to that energy after it leaves our body. There is the potential for it to go anywhere in the universe, and more importantly, affect another being, perhaps inducing in them a similar state of rage. Let us instead take a step back and examine what we broadcast through our energetic field.

Additionally, let us look at what our nation as a whole broadcasts to the rest of the world and what sort of influence we project. In our meditation this week we want to become more conscious of the energy we send out through our thoughts, words, and actions. We want to increase our awareness of our impact on others and in doing so make a concerted effort to broadcast more positive ripples of influence as individuals and as a nation.

Week Forty-Four

Integrity and Ethics

In every successive election season the volume of negative campaign ads appears to skyrocket. These can be incredibly irritating and further make you question what value they offer. They certainly do not educate voters in any helpful way and instead seem to only reflect a lack of integrity and ethics. What an improvement would result if candidates spent their campaign funds on ads that instead helped inform voters on the key issues and also made clear their stance on those matters. If candidates were unable to clearly promote their views in a manner that did not malign their opponents they should be required to donate those advertising funds to a charitable cause. While this is likely unrealistic it also raises the question of how these candidates subsequently will behave once elected into office. Those who resort to the dirtiest of campaigns may also be prone to dispensing their elected duties with a similar disregard for integrity and ethics once in office. This week we want to focus our prayer and meditation efforts on asking that citizens appreciate the value of integrity and ethics in assessing candidates and choose wisely. Additionally, let us ask that those who are elected recognize the importance of integrity and ethics and make these qualities an integral part of service to their constituents.

Week Forty-Five

Discernment

All too often political disagreements seem fueled by rhetoric and misinformation. Periodically this seems aimed at only creating fear and anxiety among citizens concerned about proposed changes in legislation. The final version of any such changes ultimately comes down to a collaborative effort between Congress and the President. Frequently it ends up containing aspects that reflect the compromises necessary to pass such legislation. In other words, there are likely to be features that please some people but upset others. When potentially controversial changes are proposed we want to use the power of meditation and prayer to help cut through the misinformation and distortion so citizens can make better informed, sensible decisions and communicate them in a civil manner to their elected officials. This will help remove the nation from the place of irrational fear that prevents people from receiving information accurately. This week we want to assist them in clearer understanding of what is being proposed and the ability to use better discernment.

Week Forty-Six

Protection

This week in our prayer and meditation efforts let us ask that our military troops currently serving around the world be protected from harm. The life-altering impact from the injuries they receive in the line of duty is difficult to comprehend. It is hard to put into words how these young souls become changed by their experiences, even if they return with no visible signs of physical injury. In asking that they be surrounded by light we want to encircle them with a field of protection that insulates not only their physical bodies but also their hearts and souls and returns them safely to their loved ones. Use the energy of your prayer and meditation to enclose our military men and women in a cocoon of light that will deflect any harm they may encounter. Let us also ask through our prayers that they be granted the courage, wisdom, and strength to carry out their mission in an effective manner that will see them return safely to their loved ones at the end of their tour.

Week Forty-Seven

Satisfaction

A story is told about a wealthy New York investor who threw a swanky party at his Fifth Avenue luxury apartment. The guest list included several famous people including Joseph Heller, author of the classic 1960's novel, "Catch-22." As the attendees moved from room to room in the vast apartment, each more lavishly decorated than the other, one of the guests turned to Heller and said, "Do you know he [referring to the investor] makes more in a month than you made with all of your royalties from Catch-22?" Heller paused and then reportedly said, "That may be, but I have something he doesn't have." "What's that?" the guest asked. "Enough," was Heller's simple response. The story may be apocryphal, but it serves to illustrate an important lesson for us all. How much do you have to have to feel a sense of abundance? What is necessary to make you satisfied or content with what you already have? In our meditation this week we want to help establish a sense of contentment, of feeling satisfied with what we already have in life. This is a shift in consciousness for many people but ultimately is fundamental to restoring our financial health as individuals and as a nation.

Week Forty-Eight

Balance

In this hectic, fast-paced world of ours many people find it challenging to maintain a balance between work and home life. Yet both of these aspects of life are necessary. For the vast majority of us, we need to work in order to have the comfort and security to enjoy life. The problem occurs when one or the other all too readily consumes us, leaving little left for the other endeavor as a result. It is also easy to experience competing sources of demand for our attention that make us feel as though we are being torn in different directions. One of life's lessons is learning how to maintain a balance between those interests. Rather than feeling as though we are precariously walking a tightrope, we would be better served if we recognize that balance does not necessarily mean perfect symmetry. There may be times when one interest or another requires more of our attention. Instead of agonizing over what may be perceived as an unfair split of our time we would find it easier to simply remain flexible. A tightrope walker does not accomplish their daring feat by staying rigidly upright as they cross between platforms. They give with the movement of the rope and the pole they carry that helps them keep their balance. This week in our prayer and meditation let us examine where in our life and our nation we may have gone out of balance and ask that we find the flexibility to help us return to that state.

Week Forty-Nine

Understanding

There is a Bible passage from Philippians that refers to "the peace of God, which passes all understanding." This passage follows one that exhorts people not to "worry over things," and the connection between the two is interesting. All too often we become stressed by feeling as though we always need to figure out or understand the circumstances in which we find ourselves. When we are unable to reach an understanding of what is going on it can be disorienting and uncomfortable. We don't like feeling as though we don't comprehend situations because it reminds us that we aren't always in control. Yet this passage makes clear that real peace comes without necessarily being able to understand. In other words, we need to comprehend and accept that we likely won't understand everything that happens in our life. Once we reach that point of acceptance life's ups and downs take less of a toll on us. With all the uncertainty in our individual lives and in the future of this country we want to ask this week in our prayer and meditation that we reach an understanding that acknowledges we aren't in control. Let us ask that the peace that "passes all understanding" fill us with serenity and extend across this entire nation.

Week Fifty

Inclusion

Just when we think we have come so far as a nation in advancing our treatment of each other and particularly in healing our long history of racial strife something happens to challenge that notion. Children are denied entry to a private pool because of their "complexion." A respected university professor has an encounter with police officers that raises questions about racial biases. In the latter case in particular there are always two sides to a story and often neither one is accurately presented to the public. The purpose of referring to these incidents is not to cast blame but to use them as signs of how far we still have to go in truly embracing those who may seem different from us. For instance, the notion of "tolerance" is a rather misleading objective when you think about it. "Tolerance" suggests having to withstand something potentially onerous. True acceptance and understanding do not come from a position of "you stay on your side of the fence, and I'll stay on mine, and together we'll agree to let each other coexist." Rather, we want to focus this week on the concept of seeking to understand and embrace those around us with different views, backgrounds, ethnicity, etc. For us to truly meet the standard of this country as a "melting pot" we want to increase our desire for inclusion for all.

Week Fifty-One

Confidence

Many of us have a natural tendency when faced with an unexpected difficulty to go immediately to worry. Frequent business travelers quickly learn what an incredible waste of energy worry can create. In a situation where travel plans are disrupted there is often little anyone can do about events such as extreme weather. You have to learn to take a deep breath and just have confidence that things will eventually work out. You can see the stress others experience, pushing them into panic mode over not being able to get somewhere, and wonder what impact that is having on their body. Even worse is the inclination to worry about problems before they materialize. Some people who don't travel frequently too easily become distressed before starting the journey with all the "what ifs" and imagining problems that may not even develop. In hindsight, we can realize how foolish we were to worry needlessly when everything inevitably works its way to a solution. When we go first to a state of worry rather than one of trust we are essentially telling the universe we don't expect to be given assistance in our life. Instead, let us try to approach life's difficulties with a sense of confidence that we will be cared for, and that in the end as said in the proverbs of folklore "this too shall pass."

Week Fifty-Two

Peace

Whenever we pause in our busy lives to celebrate holidays with family and friends certain values become even more prominent in our thoughts. We cherish our connection to others, we realize love does not require material possessions to be expressed, and we find ourselves wishing the state of calm and peace that descends over us all could be sustained throughout the year. This week's meditation focus is a simple one – we want to connect to that sense of serenity and use the power of our prayer and meditation to help infuse the energy of peace throughout our nation and the world. In our meditation efforts let us bring to mind those areas where unrest seems to dominate. There remain constant reminders in the news of how we have much work to do to quell the violence that still injures the soul of this country. For our nation to progress to a level where we can sincerely engage the rest of the world in a peaceful manner the desire for peace must permeate beyond just the confines of government in Washington. If as individuals we each carry the spirit of peace in our bodies this energy can impact the thinking and desires of those we encounter in our everyday activities. By bringing our meditative efforts to bear on the issue we can help accelerate and extend the desire for peace across the entire nation. In our prayer and meditation this week we want to deepen and extend the desire for peace across our nation and ask that the country be blanketed with a deep and abiding peace that brings respite to all.

Index

1. Possibility
2. Discipline
3. Community
4. Stewardship
5. Hope
6. Altruism
7. Service
8. Inspiration
9. Light
10. Kindness
11. Determination
12. Faith
13. Triumph
14. Resolve
15. Optimism
16. Humility
17. Passion
18. Joy
19. Groundedness
20. Resourcefulness
21. Equilibrium
22. Dedication
23. Courage
24. Pride
25. Foresight
26. Ambition
27. Authenticity

28. Liberty
29. Truth
30. Commonality
31. Virtue
32. Empathy
33. Security
34. Forgiveness
35. Effort
36. Prosperity
37. Resilience
38. Connection
39. Self-Awareness
40. Trust
41. Cooperation
42. Adaptability
43. Influence
44. Integrity & Ethics
45. Discernment
46. Protection
47. Satisfaction
48. Balance
49. Understanding
50. Inclusion
51. Confidence
52. Peace

www.ingramcontent.com/pod-product-compliance
Lightning Source LLC
Chambersburg PA
CBHW061449040426
42450CB00007B/1278